MW01363799

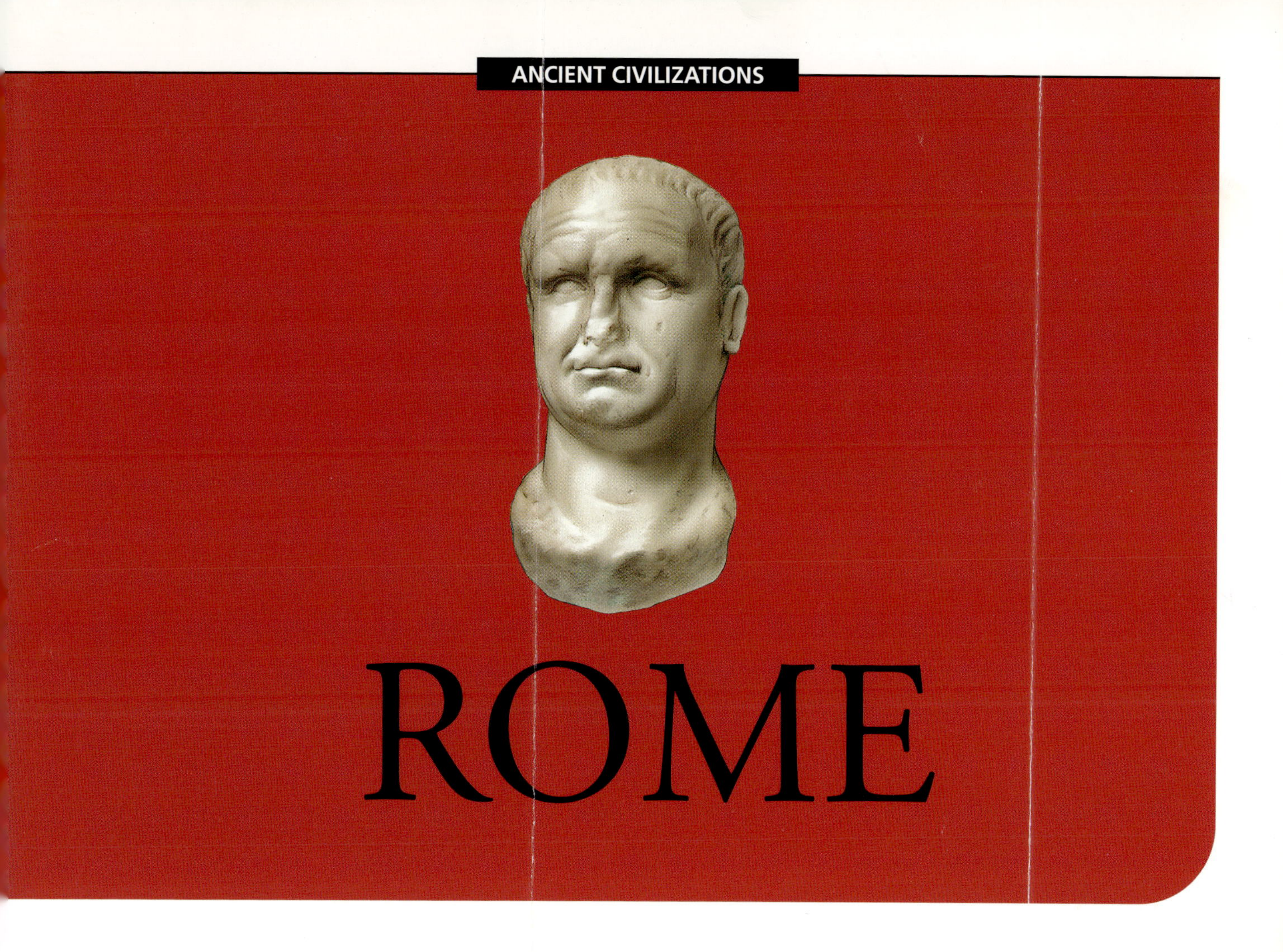

ROME

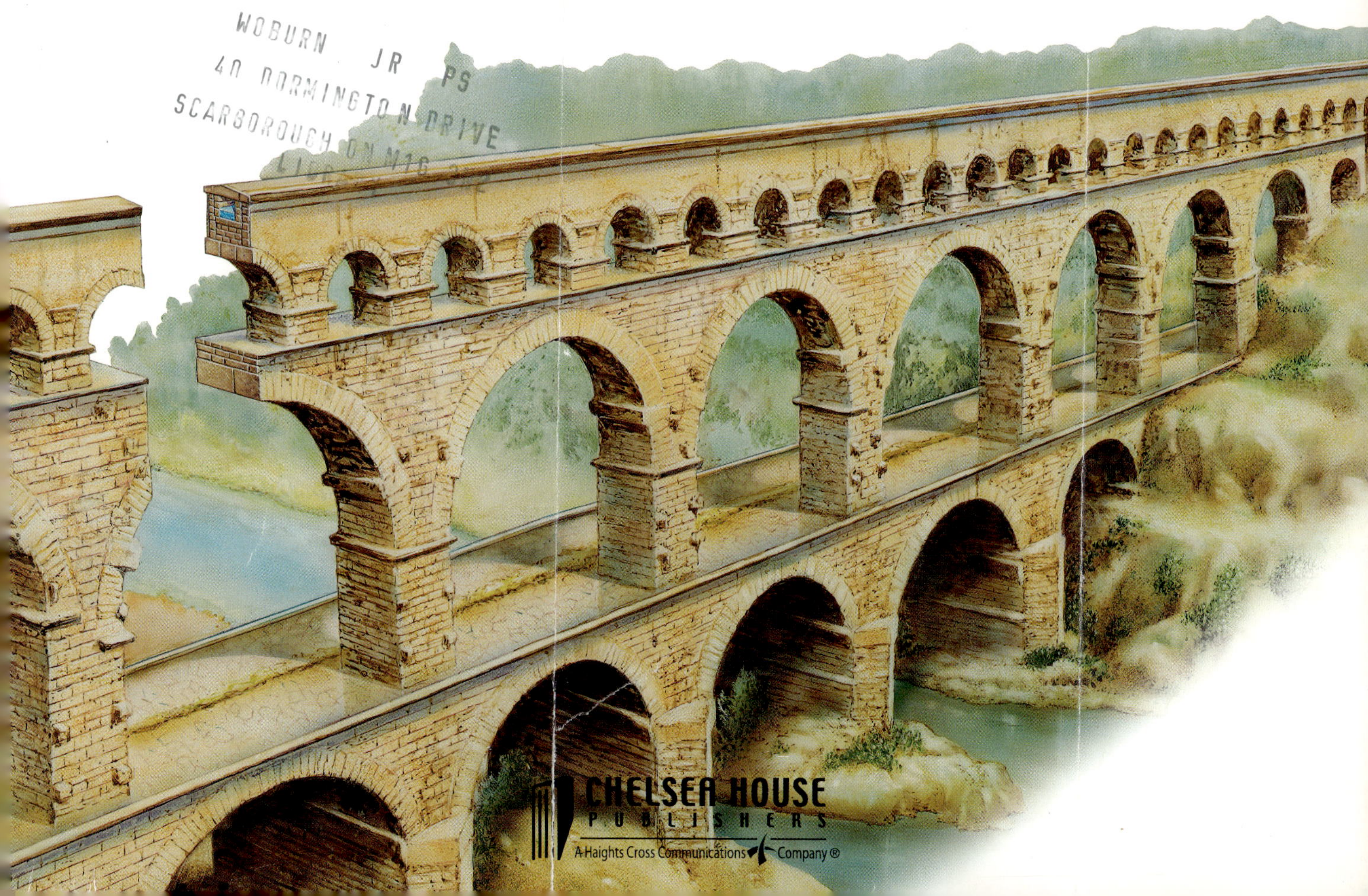

CHELSEA HOUSE
PUBLISHERS
A Haights Cross Communications Company ®

First hardcover library edition published
in the United States of America in
2006 by Chelsea House Publishers,
a subsidiary of Haights Cross Communications.

A Haights Cross Communications Company ®

www.chelseahouse.com

Library of Congress Cataloging-in-Publication Data

Bargalló i Chaves, Eva, 1960-
[Roma. English]
Rome / Eva Bargalló.
p. cm. — (Ancient civilizations)
ISBN 0-7910-8602-X (hardcover)
1. Rome—History—Juvenile literature.
I. Title. II. Ancient civilizations (Philadelphia, Pa.).
DG209.B3713 2005
937—dc22 2004027160

Project and Realization
Parramón Ediciones, S.A.

Texts
Eva Bargalló

Translator
Patrick Clark

Graphic Design and Typesetting
Estudi Toni Inglés (Alba Marco)

Illustrations
Marcel Socías Studio

First edition – February 2004

Printed in Spain

Ronda de Sant Pere, 5, 4ª planta
08010 Barcelona (España)
Empresa del Grupo Editorial Norma

www.parramon.com

TABLE OF CONTENTS

THE GREAT ROME

From the founding of Rome in the eighth century B.C., until its fall, in the fifth century A.D., one of humanity's most powerful and influential civilizations, the Roman civilization, was developed. This culture was outstanding not only for the novelty of its political institutions and the extent of its great engineering achievements, but also for the ability to bring its language, law, and art to every corner of the empire.

For all of these reasons, we want to introduce young readers to the main features of this civilization. We begin this work with a brief introduction in the form of a summary and a temporal framework for the eleven topics that will be developed in the rest of the book. These topics are guided by a short opening narrative and organized according to a central illustration that serves to explain, in a clear and concise way, different aspects of Roman culture and history as they relate to the illustration. Additional drawings also expand on the content or offer additional information.

In order to make reading easier and to complement the information provided, on the last two pages of the book we have included a glossary of terms, a brief chronology, and a list of important people in Roman history.

With regard to the selection of topics and the development of content, attractiveness and appeal took priority over exhaustiveness. Our primary objectives are to awaken in the reader an interest in the history of great civilizations without presenting confusing and excessive historical data and, at the same time, to encourage the reader to dig deeper into the material.

FROM THE SEVEN HILLS TO A GREAT EMPIRE

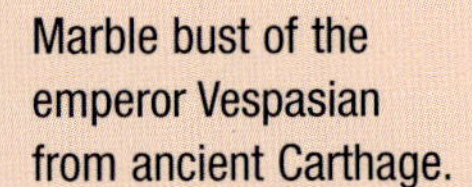

Marble bust of the emperor Vespasian from ancient Carthage.

THE MONARCHY (753–509 B.C.) THE FORMATION OF ROME

Rome, whose territory extended between the Arno and Tiber rivers and the Tyrrhenian Sea, was originally dominated by the Etruscans and its first sovereigns claimed the title of king. The Roman monarch, who enjoyed supreme power and authority to interpret the signs of the gods, did not inherit the throne, but rather was nominated by the senate and elected by the curial assemblies. These two institutions were composed of members of wealthy families or patricians.

Arch of Triumph raised over the via Augusta in the ancient Roman province of Tarracomensis, now part of the municipal terminal of Roda de Bara (Tarragon, Spain).

THE REPUBLIC (509–27 B.C.) THE DEVELOPMENT OF POLITICAL INSTITUTIONS AND BUREAUCRACY

Fearing that their monarchs would become absolute kings and that the office would become a lifetime appointment, the Romans decided to abolish the position of king, and to develop instead some institutions designed to lessen the concentration of power in a single individual and to guarantee the participation of citizens in the process of government. In this way, the senate and the curial assemblies—which in time became popular assemblies in which soldiers, peasants, and city dwellers were also represented—took on a legislative nature, and the consuls had executive powers. A complex bureaucratic and administrative network formed. The network's control extended to the most remote parts of the various provinces conquered by Rome.

In the same way, the elaboration of a legal code written in the year 450 B.C.—known as the Law of the Twelve Tablets—culminated a few centuries later with the Caracalla reform. This Reform extended the right of citizenship to all inhabitants of the empire and was a significant

The surface of the column of Trajan is covered with reliefs arranged in a spiral pattern.

milestone in the evolution of political thought and the inclusion of citizens in the decisions of the government and its institutions. Nevertheless, women and slaves were not allowed to participate in political life or hold administrative posts.

This long period was productive not only from a political and administrative point of view. From a military and colonial perspective, Rome expanded its borders from west to east and from north to south, conquering the Italian Peninsula, the ancient land of Great Greece, Spain, Greece, Carthage, Asia Minor, and Egypt.

Unfortunately, the Romans resorted to battles not only to gain new lands. Internal conflicts and disturbances also resulted in the formation of two triumvirates, in which the government of what was already a great empire fell under the control of three people. The first triumvirate, Pompey, Julius Caesar, and Crassus, ended with Caesar as dictator. He later died the victim of a conspiracy. Octavian, Marc Antony, and Lepidus formed the second triumvirate.

THE EMPIRE (27–476) AUGURS AND THE CHANCE OF A GREAT DREAM

Octavian, who succeeded in ousting the other two members of the triumvirate, was named Augustus by the senate, which eventually granted him lifelong powers. This is how the period of the republic came to an end and the period of the great emperors began.

In the year 12 B.C., the people elected Octavian Augustus to the post of Ponifex Maximus, which meant that the emperor was all-powerful. Although the institution of the senate was maintained, the title of sovereign was assumed by heredity or by adoption.

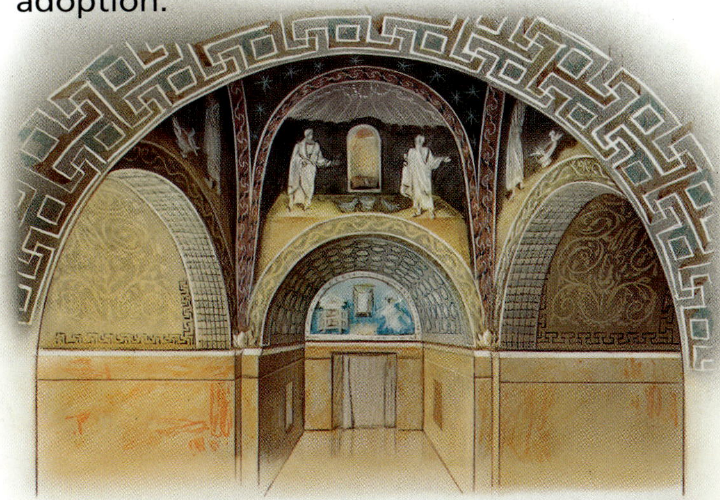

Mosaics from the mausoleum of Gala Placidia, created in the fifth century.

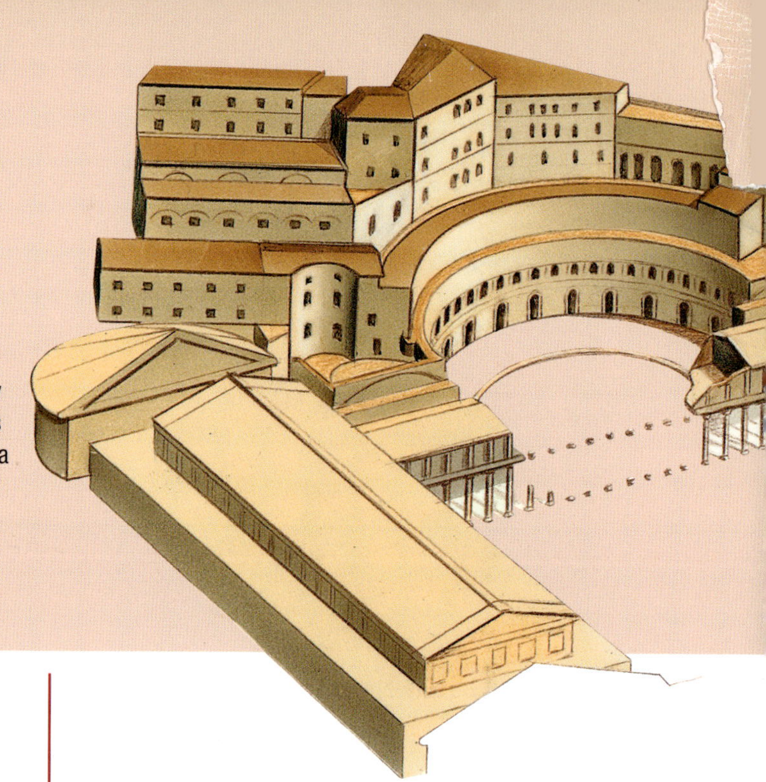

The market of Trajan, next to the forum, built by order of the emperor, was constructed according to a plan by Apollodorus of Damascus, an architect, engineer, and sculptor.

Two hundred fifty years later, abuses of power and internal conflicts compelled Diocletian to reform the system of government, and the tetrarchy was born. This means that power was divided among four people: two emperors and two consuls. However, the emperor Constantine restored the old system, once again concentrating power in the hands of a single individual.

Internal problems, as well as ever-increasing pressure by the Germanic people on the frontiers of the empire, precipitated the decline of Rome. Theodosius I divided the empire between his sons, Arcadius and Honorarius, offering to the first the Eastern Empire, whose capital was Constantinople, and granting the Western Empire to the second.

Rome, the Eternal City, was replaced by Ravenna as capital of the Western Empire, and subsequently devastated by the Germanic tribes in the year 410. Sixty-six more years would pass before Romulus Augustulus, the last emperor of the Western Empire, would be deposed by the barbarian prince Odoacrus, putting an end to one of the most brilliant chapters in the history of human civilization.

THE PLASTIC ARTS

The influence of the Greeks on Roman plastic arts and architecture was very pronounced, so much so that the Romans made copies of Greek sculptures and borrowed the great architectural orders of the Greeks: Doric, Ionic, and Corinthian.

The great contributions of the Romans to plastic arts were the portrait and the bas-relief and the introduction of figurative elements into architectural and landscape environments, combined with a profound sense of depth and perspective.

The villa of Hadrian, in Tivoli, was ordered built by the emperor Hadrian as an imperial residence.

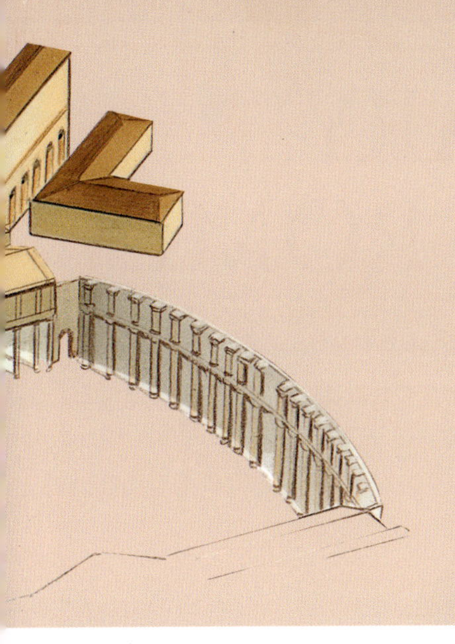

In addition to adopting Greek orders, the Romans used a new order: the Tuscan order, which is characterized by a simple column head and a smooth column (left). They also created a new type of base: the composite, a combination of the Greek Ionic and Corinthian (right).

In the area of sculpture, the great portrait artists reached such a level of perfection that they were able not only to faithfully reproduce the facial characteristics of their models, but also to convey a sense of their personalities. This careful attention to the study of the human face can also be seen in the coins that commemorated the emperors; although people appear in profile, an attempt to capture the psychology of the person can be seen.

With regard to reliefs, these covered the surfaces of columns, arches of triumph, temples, and memorial stones. Subject matter varied according to location, although the most common themes were mythological or depicted battles or memorable events for the rulers.

In the first century A.D., the interiors of residences and public buildings were decorated with fresco paintings. The themes depicted were varied, although mythological recreations dominated. The incorporation of landscapes and architectural elements provided a sense of depth and perspective to these scenes.

The mosaics that covered floors and walls evolved from two-colored and two-dimensional representations to the depiction of volume and the creation of *chiaroscuro*. Many of the compositions that have been preserved enable us to learn about the daily lives of the Romans, including their decorative preferences and customs.

PUBLIC ARCHITECTURE AND PRIVATE ARCHITECTURE

The Romans took advantage of elements from previous cultures in order to create a functional and monumental architecture. From the Greeks, they adopted the idea of architectural orders and architrave structure; from the Mesopotamians and the Etruscans, they adopted the arch and the arcade respectively.

The Romans combined and perfected all of these elements to create new structures and public buildings, such as aqueducts, triumphal arches, basilicas, and amphitheaters. Similarly, they planned their houses with the comfort of the inhabitants in mind, and constructed numerous public baths throughout the empire in order to enjoy the pleasure of water, leisure, and conversation.

THE LEGENDARY FOUNDATION OF ROME

According to legend, two brothers, sons of the god Mars and of Rhea Silvia, were thrown into the Tiber River. As luck would have it, the waters of this river deposited them at the feet of the Palatine Hills, where a she-wolf discovered them and nursed them. Years later, the twins, grandsons of Numitor, king of Alba Longa, who had been deposed by his brother Amulius, restored their grandfather to the throne and decided to found a new city: Rome. Romulus killed his brother over a disagreement about the location of the city, and the city extended to the feet of the Palatine Hills.

■ the Seven Hills
in reality, Rome emerged from the annexation of the towns built in the Seven Hills to the south of the Tiber River: Capitoline, Quirinale, Viminale, Esquiline, Caelian, Aventine, and Palatine

The Etruscans and the afterlife

The sarcophagi, the reliefs, and the paintings that decorate Etruscan funereal construction all reflect the idea of a pleasant and agreeable life after death. The image above, from the sarcophagus of Cerveteri, shows a married couple lying on a bed.

■ the Etruscans
came from Asia Minor to invade the Tiber Valley in the seventh century B.C.; their domination over Rome lasted some 150 years

■ the abduction of Sabine women
legend says that Romulus stole Sabine women in order to populate Rome; this incident resulted in a war that ended with the union of the two groups of people

■ Romulus
mythical figure who is said to have founded Rome and served as its first king; after his mysterious disappearance, he was proclaimed to be a god

■ senate

because of the growth of the city, the king had to delegate his responsibilities to a council of elders made up of descendents from the original families of Rome

■ the Etruscan mystery

numerous Etruscan funerary inscriptions have been preserved; they are written from right to left in an alphabet similar to Greek; unfortunately, their meaning is still not completely understood

The Capitoline wolf ■

this sculpture, which represents the she-wolf that nurtured Romulus and Remus, was created by the Etruscans in the fifth century B.C.

THE ROMAN MONARCHY

During this period, the monarchy was not hereditary; rather, the future sovereign was nominated by the senate and elected by the curial assembly. The king had supreme authority.

Romulus: 753 – 716 B.C.
Numa Pompilius: 716 – 673 B.C.
Tulius Hostilius: 673 – 641 B.C.
Ancius Marcius: 641 – 616 B.C.
Lucius Tarquinius Priscus: 616 – 578 B.C.
Servius Tullius: 578 – 534 B.C.
Lucius Tarquinius: 534 – 509 B.C.

THE FORUM, CENTER OF POLITICAL LIFE

Did you know that the word "republic" comes from the Latin expression "*res publica*," which means "public affairs"? In the year 509 B.C., Rome brings the monarchy to an end and embarks on a new kind of government, the republic, whose institutions were created with the intention of sharing power, and in this way avoiding the abuse of authority. The position of king is replaced by two consuls. They command the army and are elected annually.

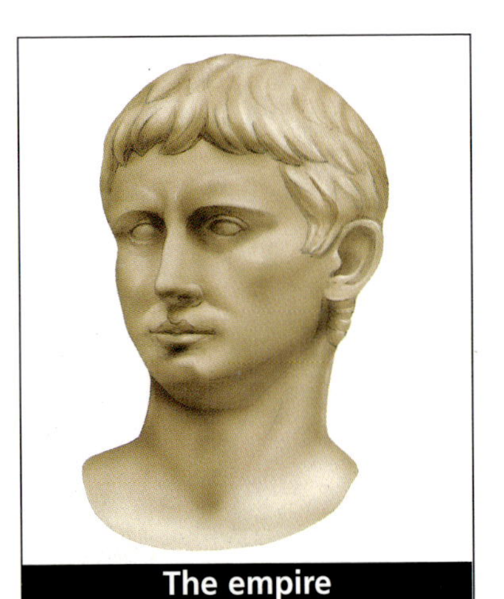

The empire

It begins in the year 10 A.D. when Octavian is named Augustus and granted lifelong powers by the senate. In this way, the title of emperor, which means "he that commands" in Latin, becomes a hereditary title.

■ **senate**
originally consisted of 300 senators who deliberated and passed judgment on big political decisions

forum ■
the nerve center of Roman cities. The most representative government buildings of the city were built around it

■ **magistracy**
formed by high officials (two consuls, two praetors, two censors, four aediles, and four quaestors) who administered and directed policy

■ **consuls**
commanded the army and fulfilled functions as judges and directors of the public treasury

■ **praetors**
magistrates who acted as judges among citizens, and between citizens and foreigners

A TRADITIONAL SOCIETY

Noble familes (*gens*), who took charge of political responsibilities and high military commands, dominated Roman society. Slaves were called *libertos* when their masters granted them freedom. Free people, who were under the protection of a *pater*, the chief of the *gens*, were called clients. Plebians were individuals who did not belong to any family.

■ censors
these officials conducted censuses of the population, kept track of goods, and watched over public customs

■ aediles
in charge of inspecting marketplaces and watching over public actions

■ quaestors
responsible for administering government income and expenditures

■ committees
assemblies made up of citizens for the purpose of electing magistrates

■ dictator
in the event of war, an elected magistrate for an unspecified period of time, had full power and authority

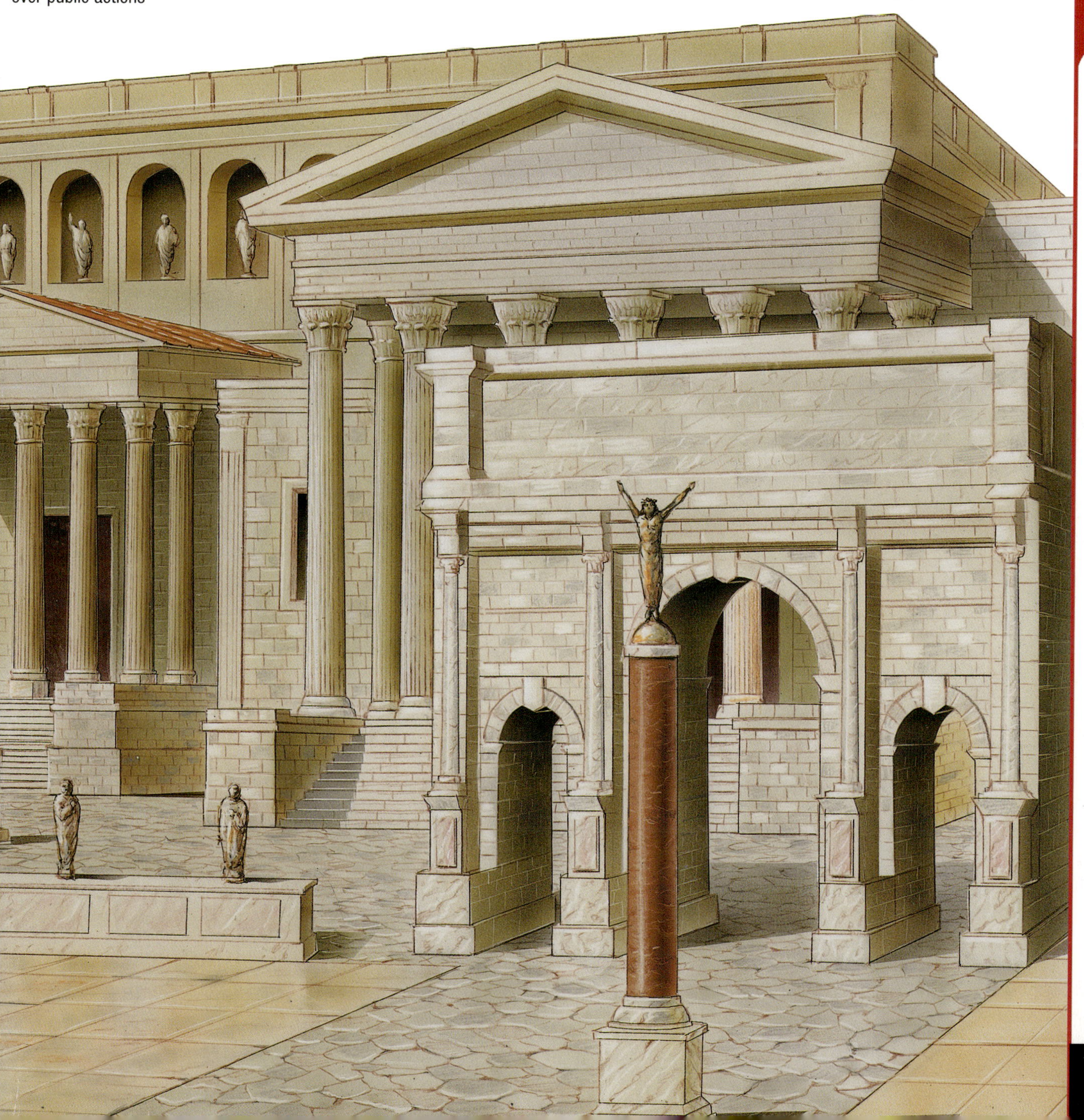

IN THE SERVICE OF WAR

What was the legion? In ancient Rome, the main body of the best-prepared army of the world was known by this name. As a general rule, the army consisted of four legions. Each legion was composed of more than five thousand soldiers and divided into ten groups called cohorts. These, in turn, were divided into six centuries, each one commanded by a centurion. Each century was divided into ten *contuberniums*, which were the minimum units of the army. Legionaires began their military careers as simple infantry soldiers.

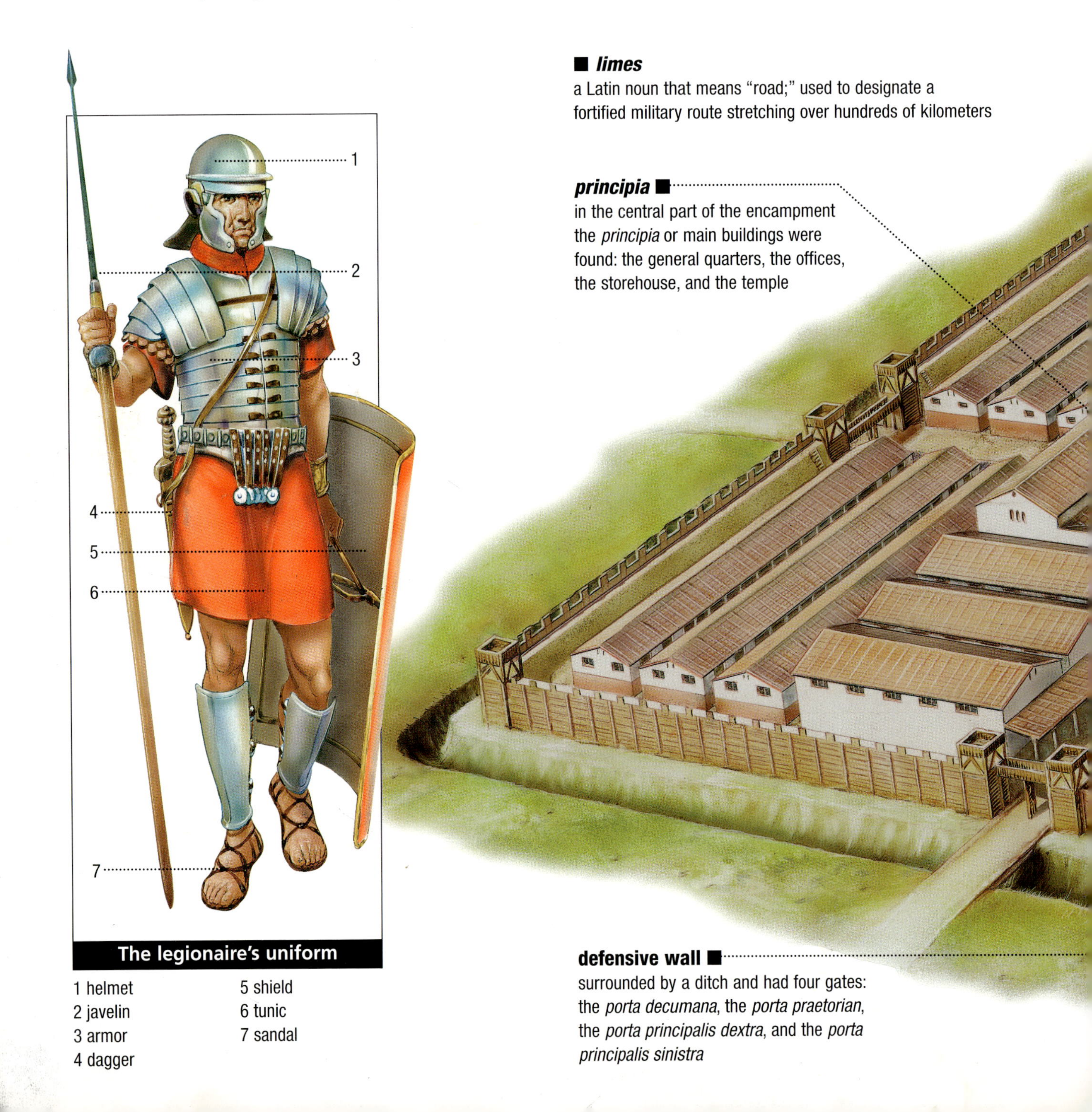
1
2
3
4
5
6
7
limes
a Latin noun that means "road;" used to designate a fortified military route stretching over hundreds of kilometers
principia
in the central part of the encampment the *principia* or main buildings were found: the general quarters, the offices, the storehouse, and the temple
defensive wall
surrounded by a ditch and had four gates: the *porta decumana*, the *porta praetorian*, the *porta principalis dextra*, and the *porta principalis sinistra*

The legionaire's uniform

1 helmet
2 javelin
3 armor
4 dagger
5 shield
6 tunic
7 sandal

BATTLE FOR DOMINATION OF THE MEDITERRANEAN

During the Punic Wars, the Romans and Carthaginians battled over commercial sovereignty of *Mare Nostrum*. The Romans emerged victorious in all three wars. In the last one, after three long years of fighting, the Carthaginians were definitively beaten, and the city of Carthage was set on fire.

■ **catapult**
war machine used by the Romans to launch huge stones at the enemy

■ ***imperator***
the person who exercised supreme authority in controlling the troops in the Roman army

standard ■
every legion had its own standard or insignia, which was carried by the standard bearer

cardo ■
main street that ran north to south

■ ***decumano***
main street that ran east to west

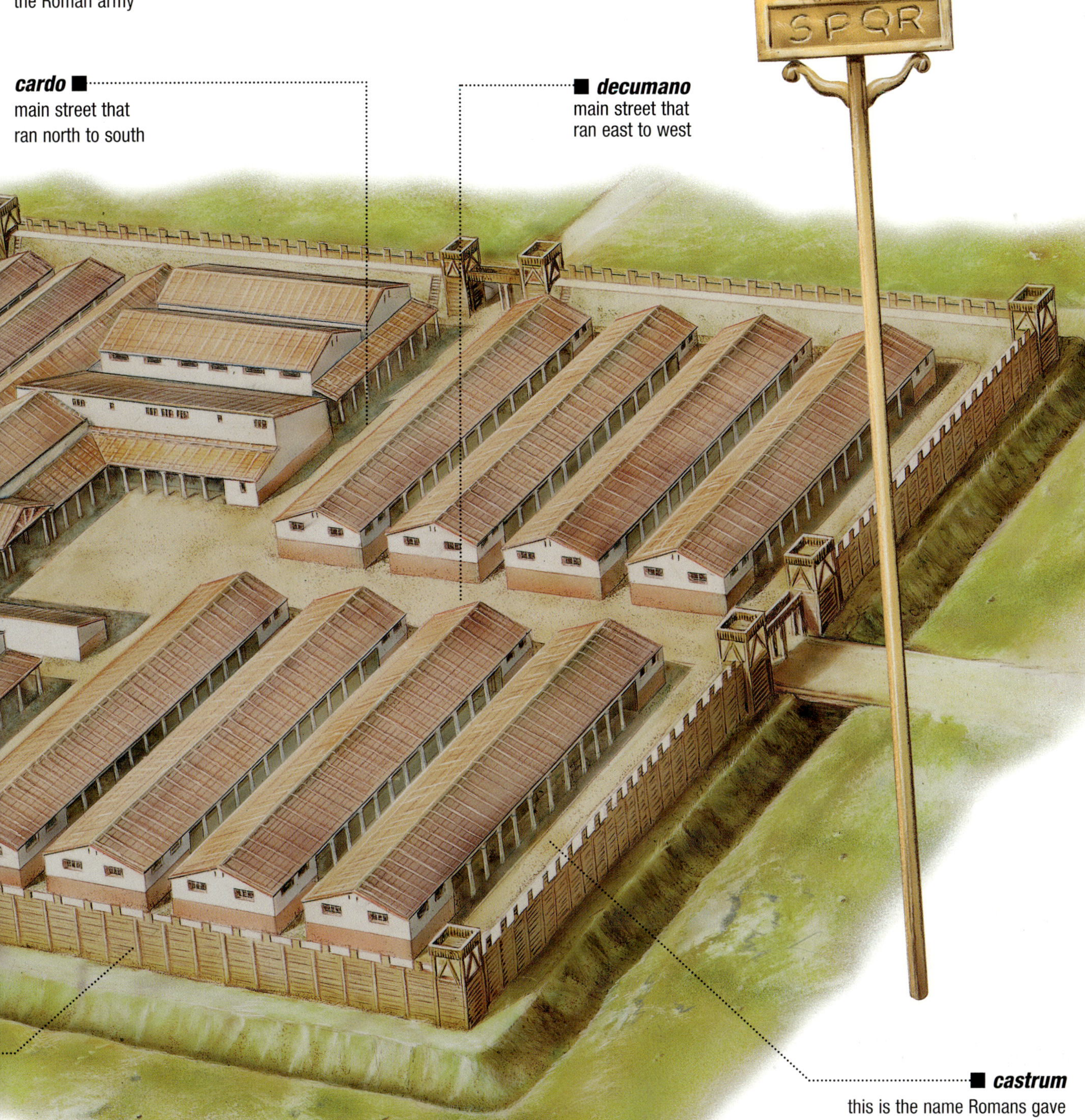
SPQR

■ ***castrum***
this is the name Romans gave to military encampments constructed to hold the troops

A CONQUERING PEOPLE

The Romans built a fabulous empire. From the third century B.C., when they dominated the Italian Peninsula, until the second century A.D., a time of the greatest expansion of the imperial frontiers, the City of the Seven Hills was able, thanks to brilliant strategists such as the great Julius Caesar, and with the help of a powerful army, to dominate from the extreme north of Africa to the Iberian Peninsula and Great Britain, and from the Atlantic Ocean to the Caspian Sea. But the Romans stood out not only for their ability to conquer, but also for the will to Romanize the territories they occupied, and to bring to any place in the empire the culture, laws, and especially, the civilization of Rome.

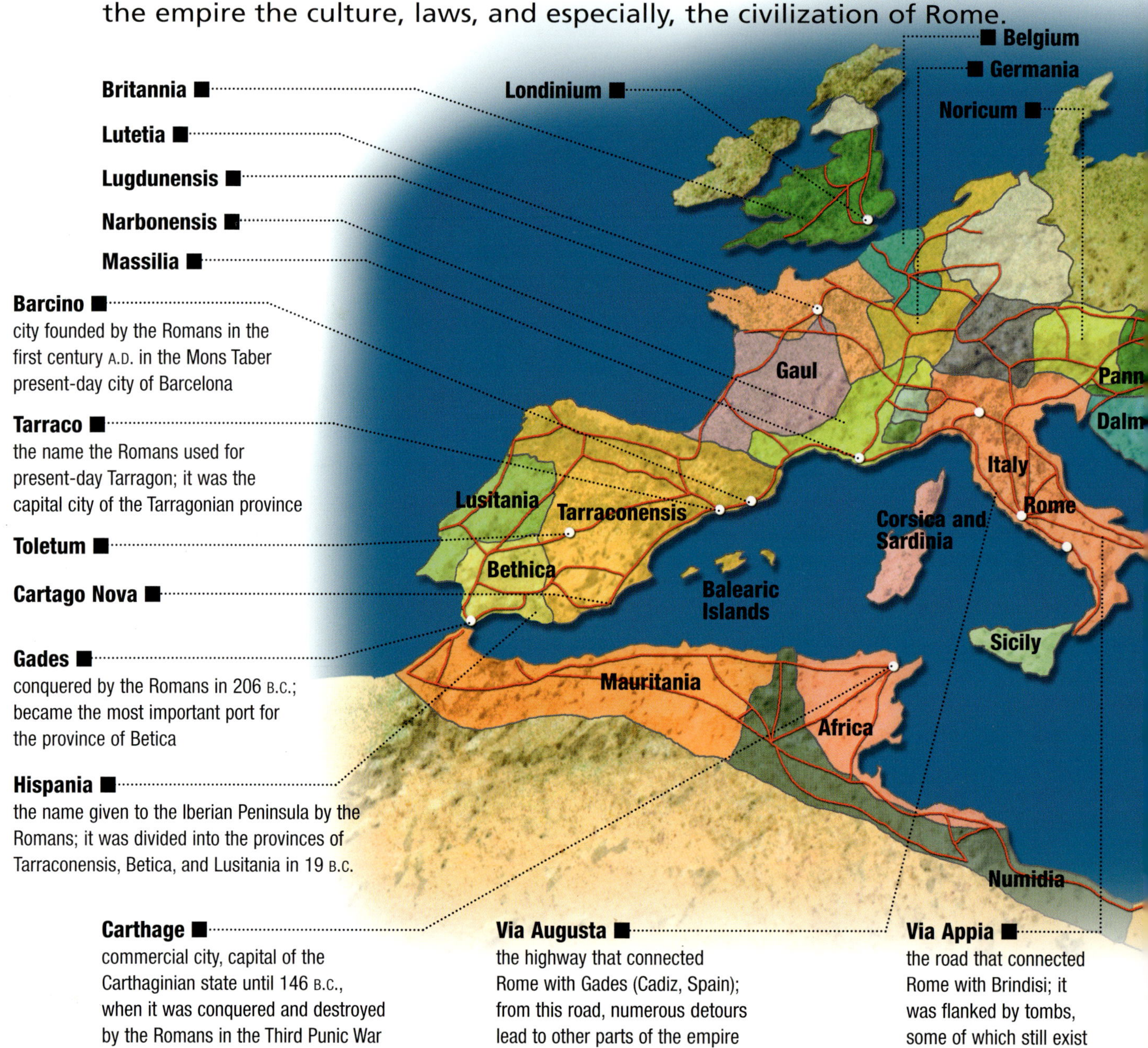
Britannia
Lutetia
Lugdunensis
Narbonensis
Massilia
Barcino
city founded by the Romans in the first century A.D. in the Mons Taber present-day city of Barcelona
Tarraco
the name the Romans used for present-day Tarragon; it was the capital city of the Tarragonian province
Toletum
Cartago Nova
Gades
conquered by the Romans in 206 B.C.; became the most important port for the province of Betica
Hispania
the name given to the Iberian Peninsula by the Romans; it was divided into the provinces of Tarraconensis, Betica, and Lusitania in 19 B.C.
Londinium
Belgium
Germania
Noricum
Gaul
Pann
Dalm
Italy
Rome
Corsica and Sardinia
Lusitania
Tarraconensis
Bethica
Balearic Islands
Sicily
Mauritania
Africa
Numidia
Carthage
commercial city, capital of the Carthaginian state until 146 B.C., when it was conquered and destroyed by the Romans in the Third Punic War
Via Augusta
the highway that connected Rome with Gades (Cadiz, Spain); from this road, numerous detours lead to other parts of the empire
Via Appia
the road that connected Rome with Brindisi; it was flanked by tombs, some of which still exist

THE JULIAN CALENDAR

In 46 B.C., Julius Caesar changed the Roman calendar. Every year would have 365 days, except for leap years, which would have 366. In our calendar, every year is divided into twelve months: January, March, May, July, August, October, and December have thirty-one days; most others have thirty days; February, has twenty-eight days in normal years, and twenty-nine in leap years.

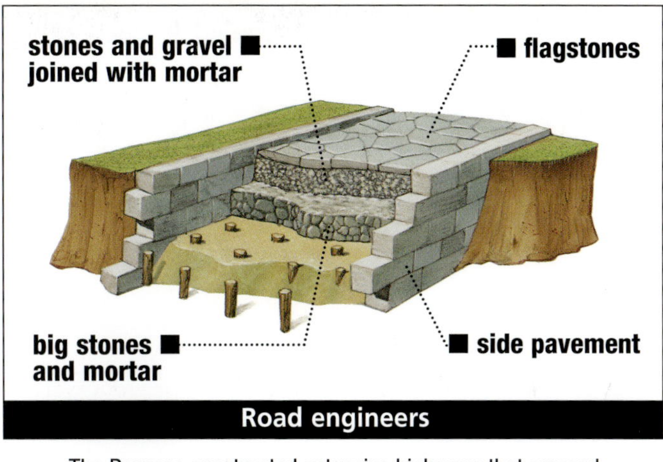
stones and gravel joined with mortar
flagstones
big stones and mortar
side pavement

Road engineers

The Romans constructed extensive highways that crossed the empire with big flagstones that rested on various layers of gravel and stones held together with mortar. They protected the sides of the road with big blocks of stone.

■ **roads**
the Romans constructed more than 4,722 miles (7,600 kilometers) of highways to make communication easier between different provinces of the empire

■ **province**
the Romans divided the territories they conquered into provinces that fell under the jurisdiction of a Roman magistrate

■ **Constantinople**
the emperor Constantine ordered this city built on the ruins of ancient Byzantium; in 395 A.D., when the Roman Empire was divided, this city became the capital of the Eastern Empire

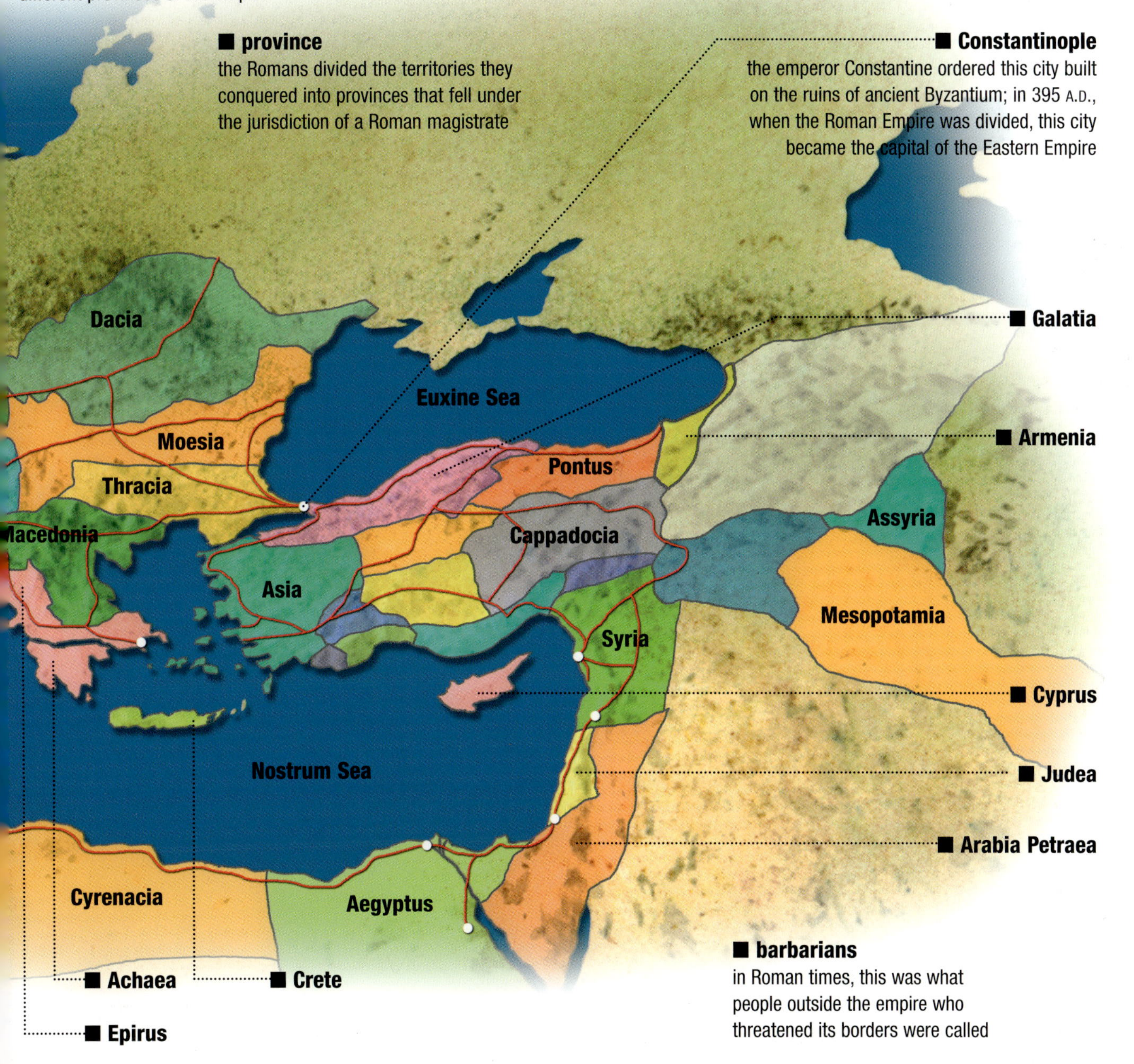
Dacia
Euxine Sea
Moesia
Thracia
Macedonia
Pontus
Cappadocia
Asia
Syria
Assyria
Mesopotamia
Nostrum Sea
Cyrenacia
Aegyptus
Galatia
Armenia
Cyprus
Judea
Arabia Petraea
Achaea
Crete
Epirus

■ **barbarians**
in Roman times, this was what people outside the empire who threatened its borders were called

ONE LANGUAGE FOR THE WHOLE EMPIRE

What do Spanish, Catalan, Gallego, French, and Italian have in common? They are all derived from the same language, Latin, which was used in all the provinces of Rome. Its influence was so great that it survived the fall of the Roman Empire in the fifth century A.D., and evolved over time into other languages called Romance languages. This beautiful language was used by the Romans not only as a means of communication, but also to make laws, to create a rich literature, and to write eloquently about philosophy, history, or politics.

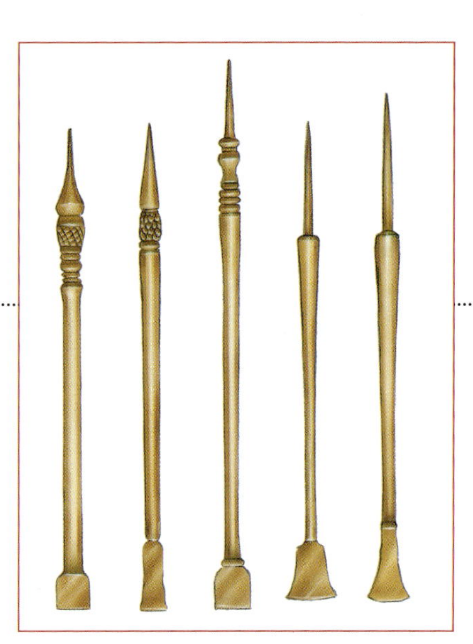

stylus ■ implement for writing on soft materials such as wax; its elongated shape ended in a sharp tip on one side, and a flat spatula on the other to erase

tabulae ■ tablets, normally made of wood and covered with wax, that could be used for writing with a stylus; sometimes they were covered with a layer of plaster, in order to write with a *calamus* (reed) and ink

ROMANIZATION

The Romans imposed their institutions, their laws, their language, and their culture on all the territories of the empire. Commercial relations, together with a wide communications network, facilitated this phenomenon, known as Romanization.

■ Maecenas

this was the name of an advisor to Octavian Augustus, the emperor whose mission was to protect writers and artists; his name became synonymous with the idea of an individual artist gaining patronage and protection

■ literary forms

Roman writers used all the literary genres created or developed by the Greeks: theater (Plautus), oratory (Cicero), poetry (Virgil, Ovid), and history (Livy), etc.

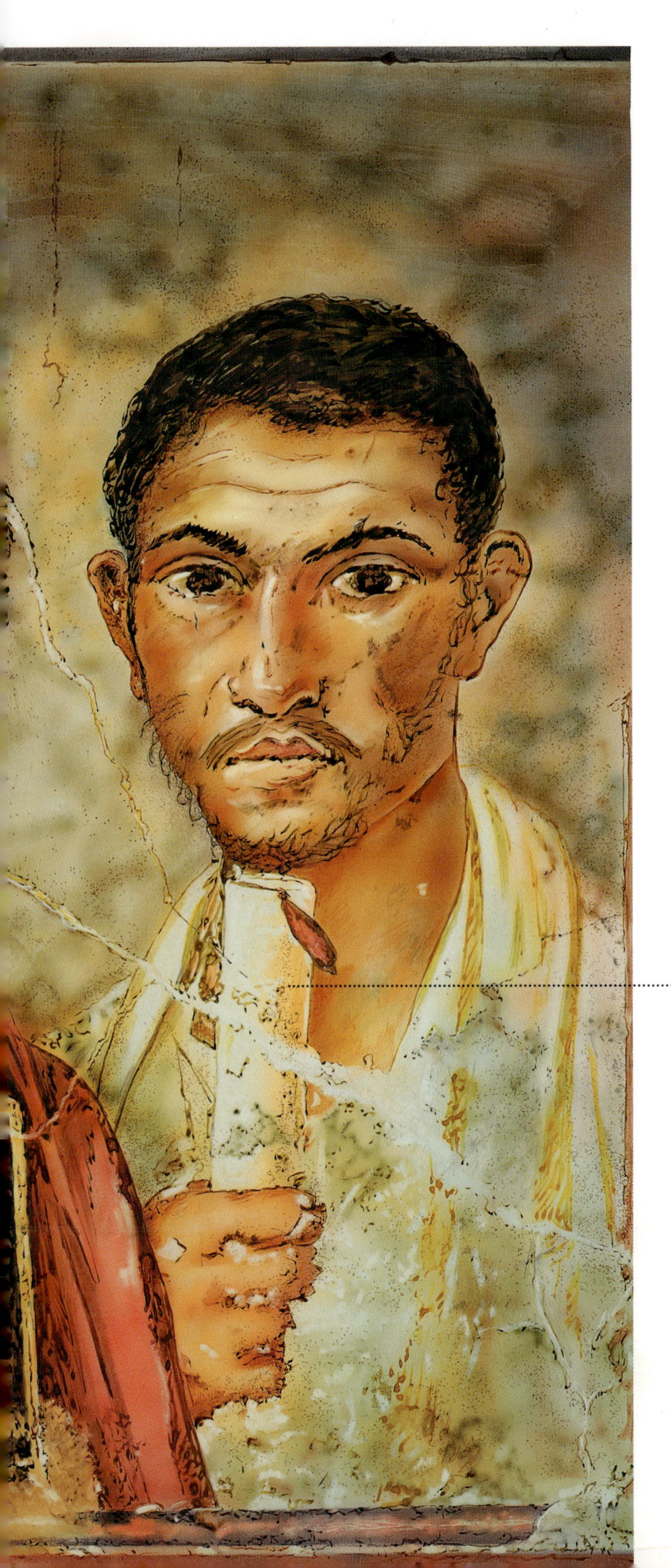

IDALIAELVCOSVBIM
FLORIBVSETDVLCIAD
IAMQ·IBATDICTOPAR

Capital letters (upper-case)

Curial letters (lower-case)

The Latin alphabet

The Romans adapted the Etruscan alphabet. The thing that was written upon could be made of anything from wood and metal to terracotta, tablets, or papyrus. Similarly, different types of letters were used, depending on the era and its customs.

■ *calamus*

a reed pen cut into a slanting point that was used as a writing implement

■ *volumen*

a set of papyrus or parchment strips rolled up in order to write a continuous text on them, in columns that continued up and down

■ *liber*

the front part of the bark of a plant where the Romans wrote; the word "library" comes from this Latin word

PATRON GODS AND OFFICIAL GODS

The Roman mythological universe was populated by all kinds of gods: gods that protected the home, gods of Greek origin, gods that were specifically Roman, deified emperors, and deities from the East around which cults and mysteries were celebrated. The emperors Constantine and Theodosius put an end to this chaos, the first by legalizing Christianity, and the second by making this new religion official.

cista

Funeral rites

The Romans practiced burial as well as incineration. In the first case, they would bury bodies in houses or gardens, until a law required the dead to be buried outside the city, in a necropolis. In incineration, the ashes of the deceased were deposited in funeral urns or *cistas*, containers made of bronze that could be different shapes.

THE UNDERGROUND WORLD OF THE CATACOMBS

The first Christians were persecuted by the Romans for standing up against paganism and official cults. On the walls of their secret meeting places, the catacombs, were praying figures and Christian symbols such as the fish. (The word "fish," in Greek, is an anagram for Christ.)

■ *mane*
in Roman households, each family honored its illustrious ancestors, the *manes*, offering sacrifices to them, and making them an object of worship

■ *lares*
divinities who protected the household, including its inhabitants, their house, and property, were known by this name

■ *penates*
genies or spirits who protected stored food

■ altar
the *pater familias* offered food sacrifices to the household gods on a small altar

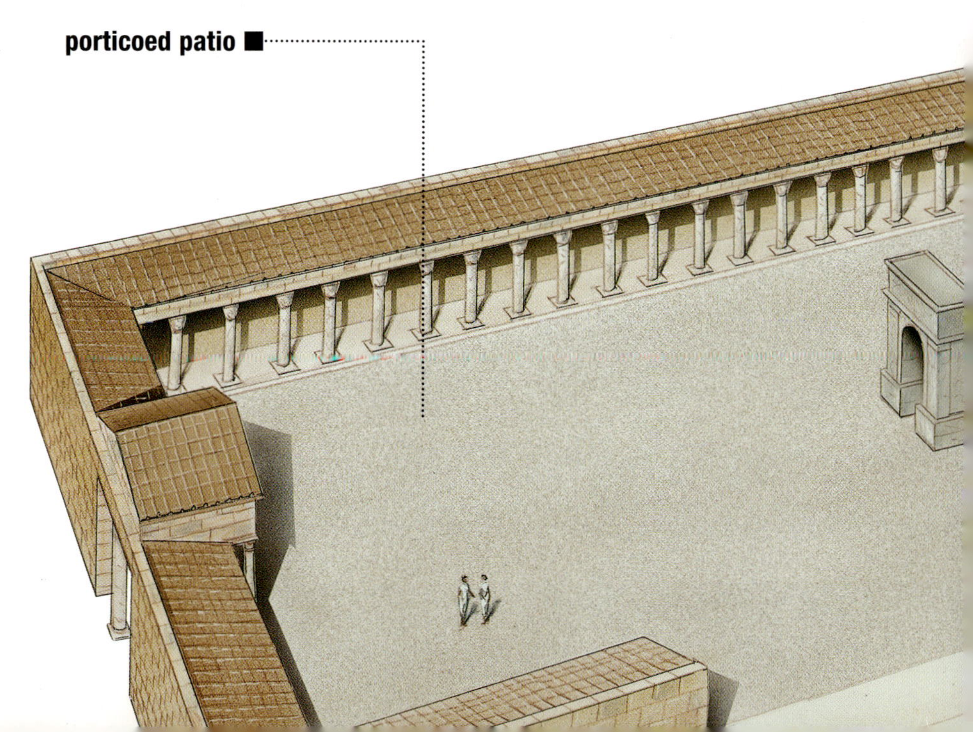
porticoed patio

Jupiter
governed as the principal god of the Roman Pantheon; he is generally shown sitting on a throne of gold, with a beam of light in one hand and a scepter in the other

Mars
god of war, son of Jupiter and Juno; he is usually depicted with the features of a young man, and dressed as a warrior

Juno
queen of the gods, goddess of heaven and earth, and protector of kingdoms and empires and sister and wife of Jupiter

Minerva
goddess of wisdom, along with the Greek goddess Athena; she came from the head of Jupiter dressed as a female warrior

Saturn
god of agriculture and symbol of time; he is usually shown as an old man carrying a sickle in one hand, a symbol that stands for the force of time that destroys everything; his other hand holds an hourglass

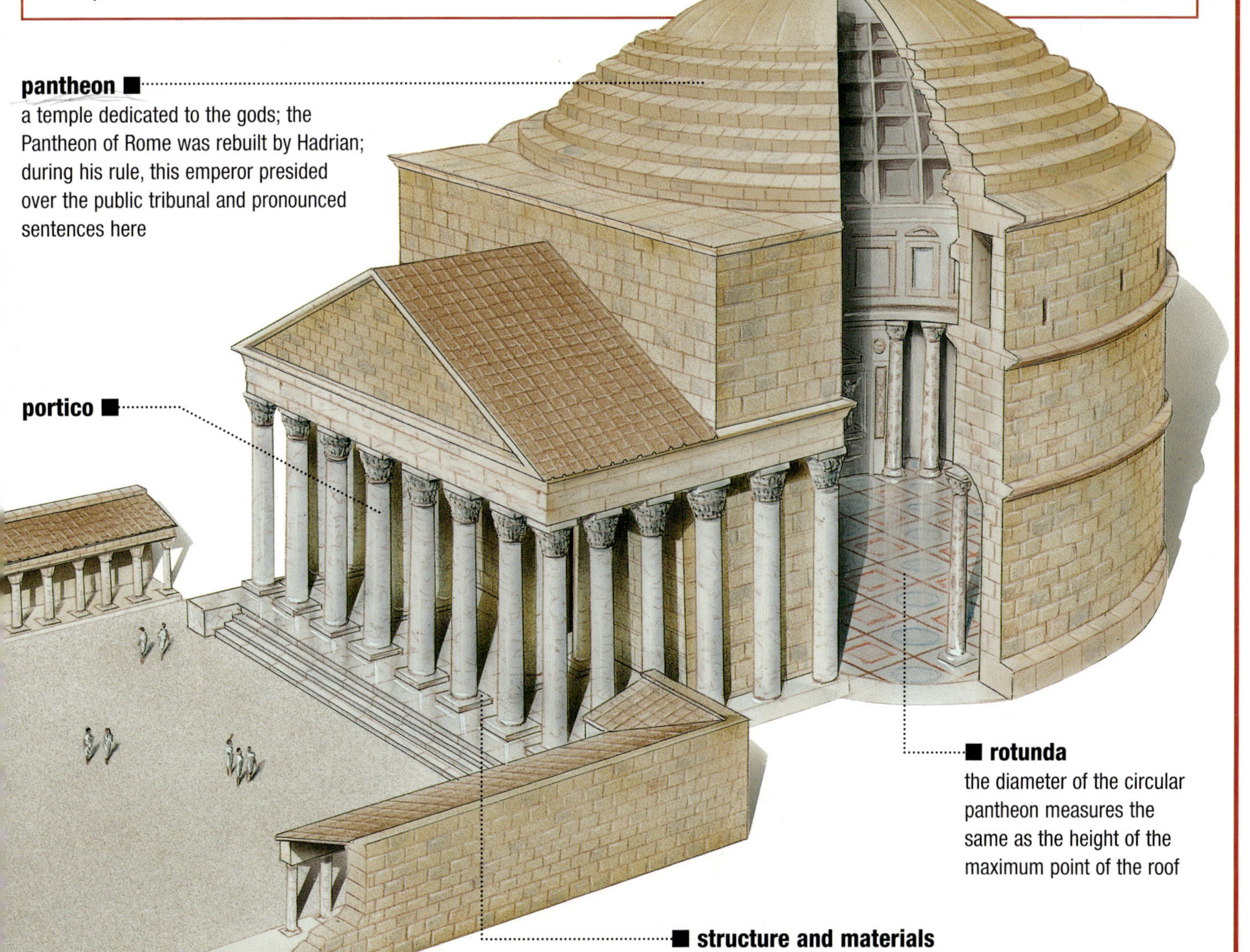

pantheon
a temple dedicated to the gods; the Pantheon of Rome was rebuilt by Hadrian; during his rule, this emperor presided over the public tribunal and pronounced sentences here

portico

rotunda
the diameter of the circular pantheon measures the same as the height of the maximum point of the roof

structure and materials
The Roman Pantheon is divided into two parts, the portico and the rotunda; different materials were used for its construction: granite and marble for the portico, and concrete for the rotunda

THE GREATEST SHOW IN THE WORLD

Roman architects were great builders of civic buildings, such as amphitheaters, theaters, pantheons, and triumphal arches. The most outstanding is the great Roman Colosseum: a magnificent amphitheater four stories high, with a circular floor plan, where fights between gladiators and with wild animals, and even big naval battles, took place. Everyone from the emperor down to the common people attended these impressive shows.

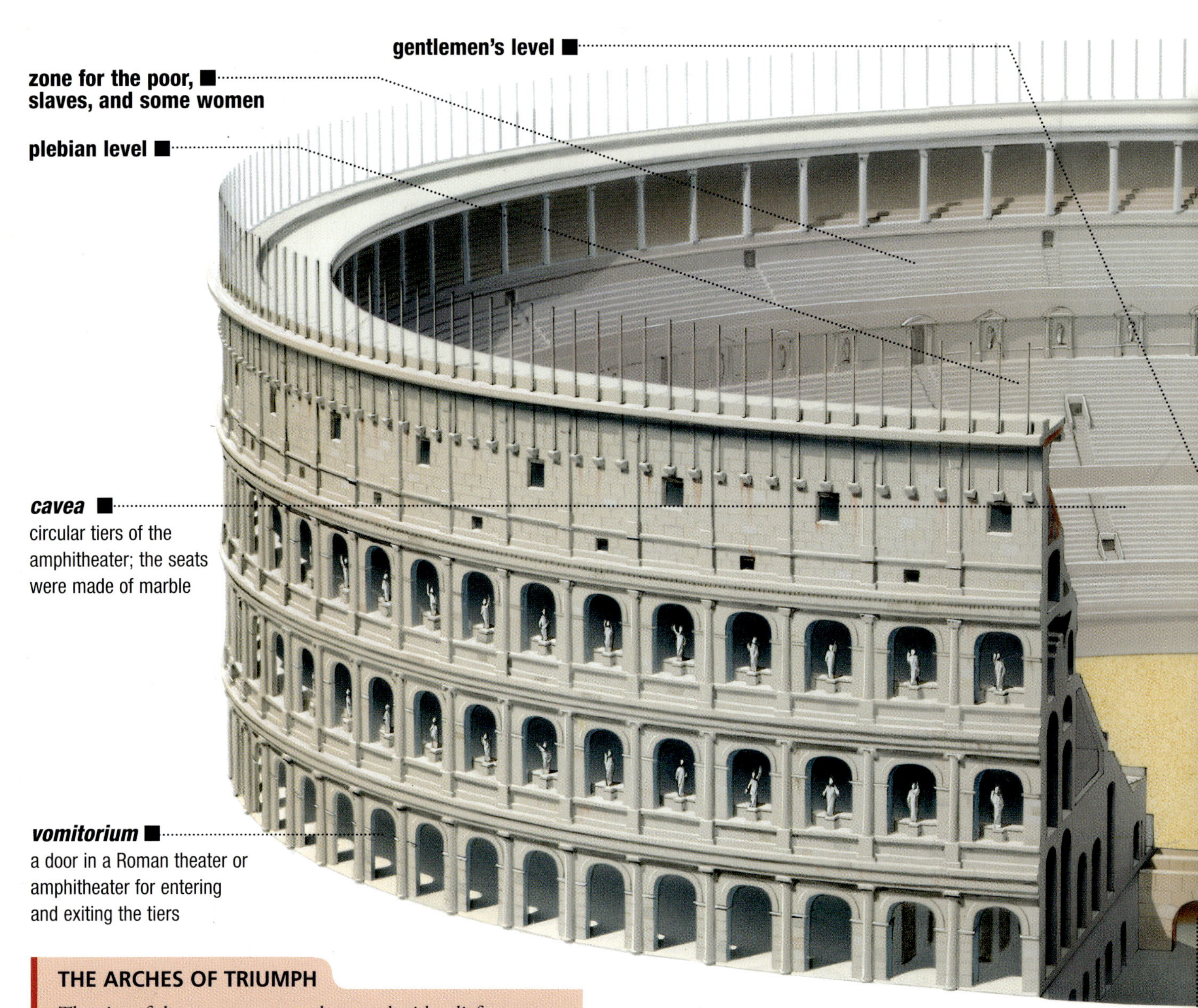
gentlemen's level
zone for the poor, slaves, and some women
plebian level
cavea
circular tiers of the amphitheater; the seats were made of marble
vomitorium
a door in a Roman theater or amphitheater for entering and exiting the tiers
underground
the structures used to house the animal cages and the changing rooms were under the arena; there was also a system of canals and drains to cover the sand

THE ARCHES OF TRIUMPH

The aim of these monuments, decorated with reliefs, was to commemorate military triumphs. The scenes depicted were typically taken from episodes related to the emperor's victories over conquered peoples.

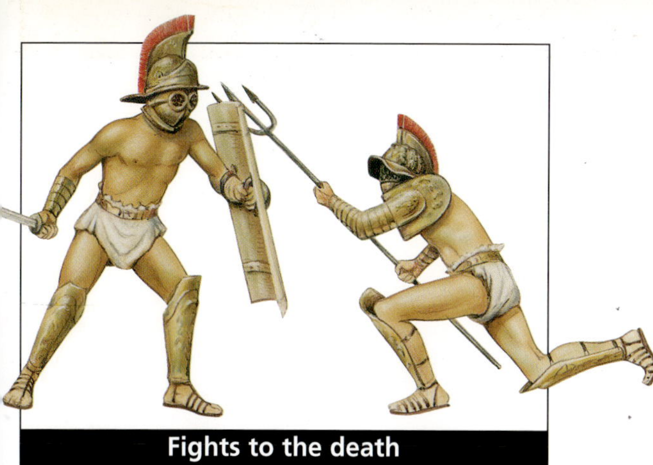

Fights to the death

The fights between gladiators were to the death. The public, and ultimately the emperor, decided the fate of a badly injured fighter. The sovereign raised or lowered his thumb to condemn or pardon him.

podium
the place reserved for the emperor and members of the most important families

zero row
the area of the first rows was reserved for people of high social status

seating capacity
the Colosseum could seat more than fifty thousand spectators

velarium
a system of awnings that hung over the rows in order to protect spectators from the rays of the sun

gladiators
professional fighters who fought in amphitheaters, in pairs or groups; they were usually slaves or prisoners of war

box seats for the consul and the vestal virgins

senators' level

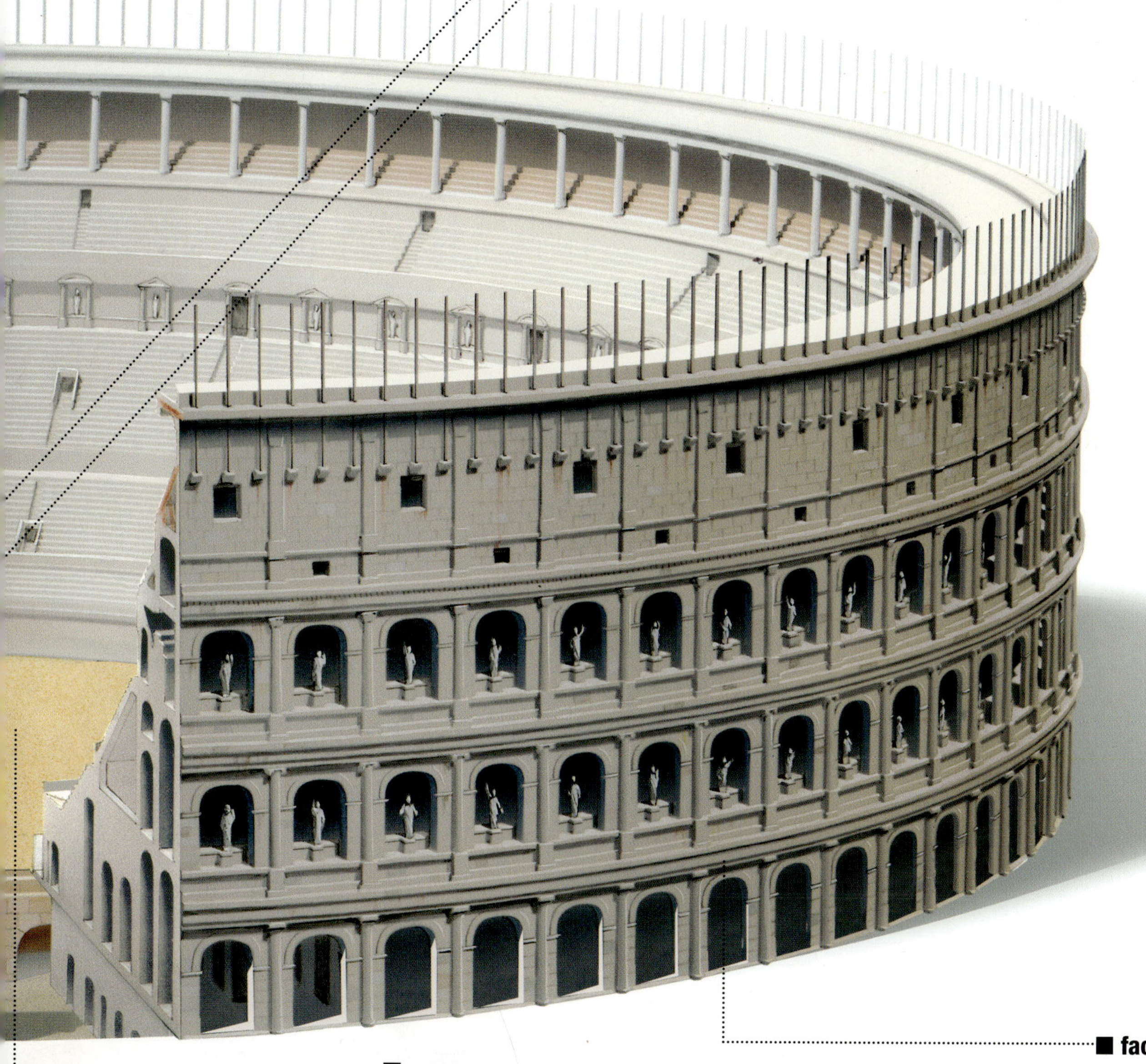

arena
the center part of the amphitheater where combats and games or shows took place; the Colosseum arena has an elliptical shape

facade
has four floors: the first three are arcaded galleries with Doric, Ionic, and Corinthian styles respectively; the fourth floor was added later

THE PASSAGEWAY FOR THE WATERS

The use of the arch, already used by the Mesopotamians and the Etruscans, allowed the Romans to develop one of the greatest engineering works of all time: the aqueduct. This succession of arches served to supply water to the cities of the empire. Some of the most important are the Pont du Gard aqueduct and the one in Segovia. In places where water was scarce, there was also a hydraulic system to gather water in the winter, with reservoirs and canals to lead them up the slopes, so no water would be lost.

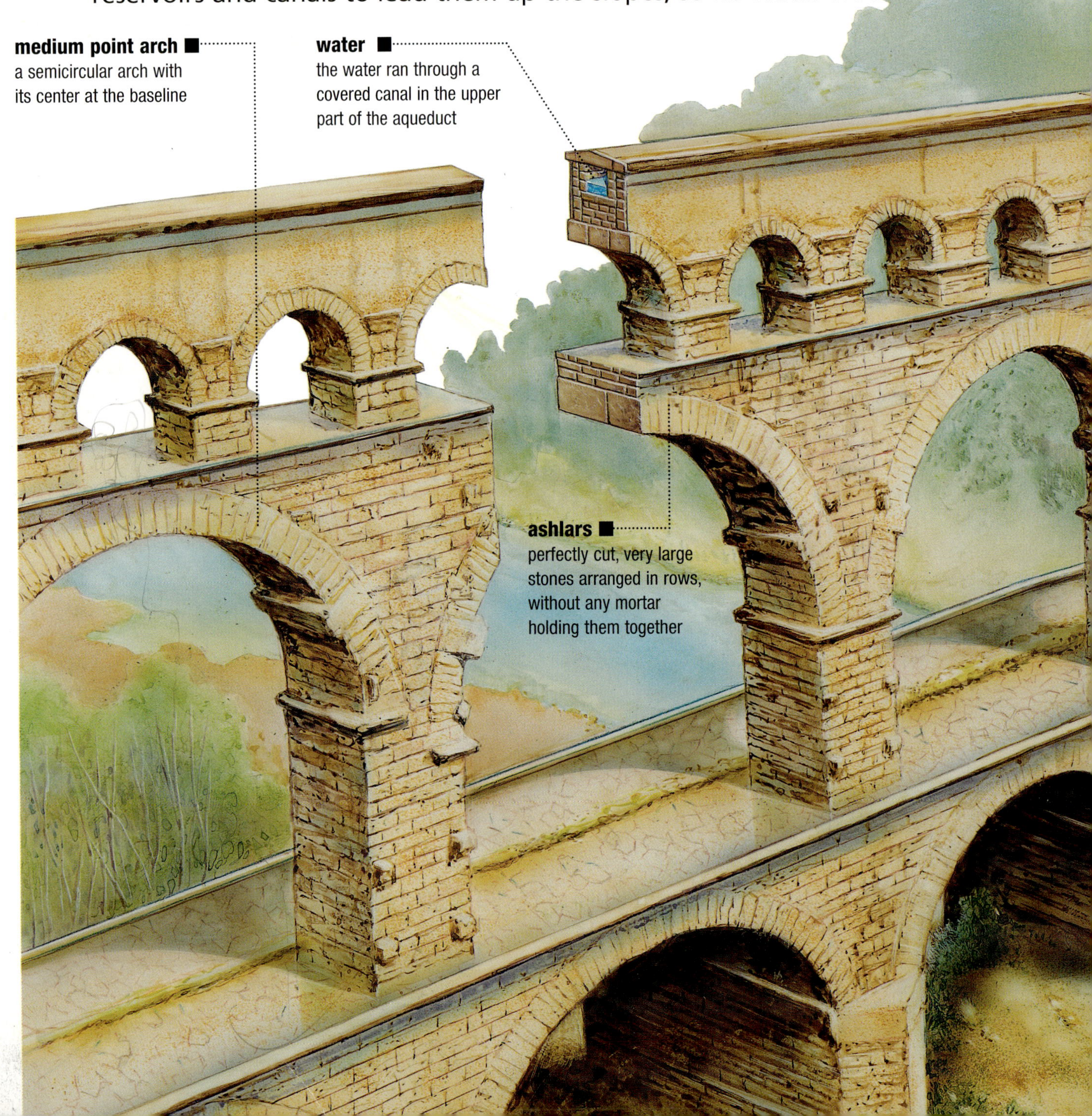
medium point arch
a semicircular arch with its center at the baseline
water
the water ran through a covered canal in the upper part of the aqueduct
ashlars
perfectly cut, very large stones arranged in rows, without any mortar holding them together

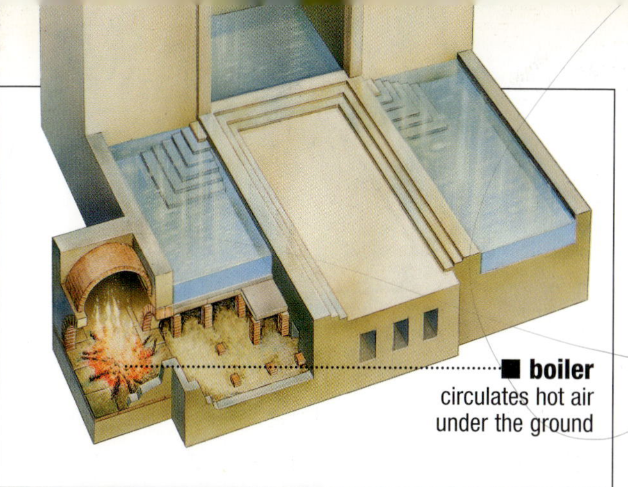
boiler
circulates hot air under the ground

The baths

These establishments were places with pools where one could take cold baths (*frigidarium*), hot baths (*caldarium*), and steam baths. In addition, there was the *tepidarium*, the rooms used for lukewarm baths, and the *natatio*, an outdoor pool.

construction system
the aqueducts were built using rows of arches that decreased in size for the terrain; they could have several levels
builders
big projects such as this required the cooperation of many overseers, as well as builders and stone masons
pillars
vertical supports with a square base; those of Pont du Gard are about thirty-three feet by about sixteen feet and support the entire structure above
Pont du Gard
this aqueduct, which also served as a bridge, provided water to the city of Nimes (France); it was 984 feet long, and attained a maximum altitude of 164 feet, and it is in perfect condition today

AQUEDUCT OF SEGOVIA

This impressive aqueduct was built in Segovia (Spain), probably during the reign of Trajan, in the first quarter of the second century. It is 2,667 feet (813 meters) long, 93.5 feet high (28.5 meters) at its highest point, and has 128 arches arranged in two levels. Until just a few years ago, it was still supplying water to the city.

A TASTE FOR COMFORT

The Romans generally lived in beautiful houses based on the Etruscan tradition. The main rooms were arranged around the atrium. Such a house was called a *domus*. However, in the big cities, due to lack of space and an increasing need for housing, *insulas*, buildings of several floors, became more popular. Aristocratic and powerful families had second residences built for themselves, far from the concentration of population. These were called villas.

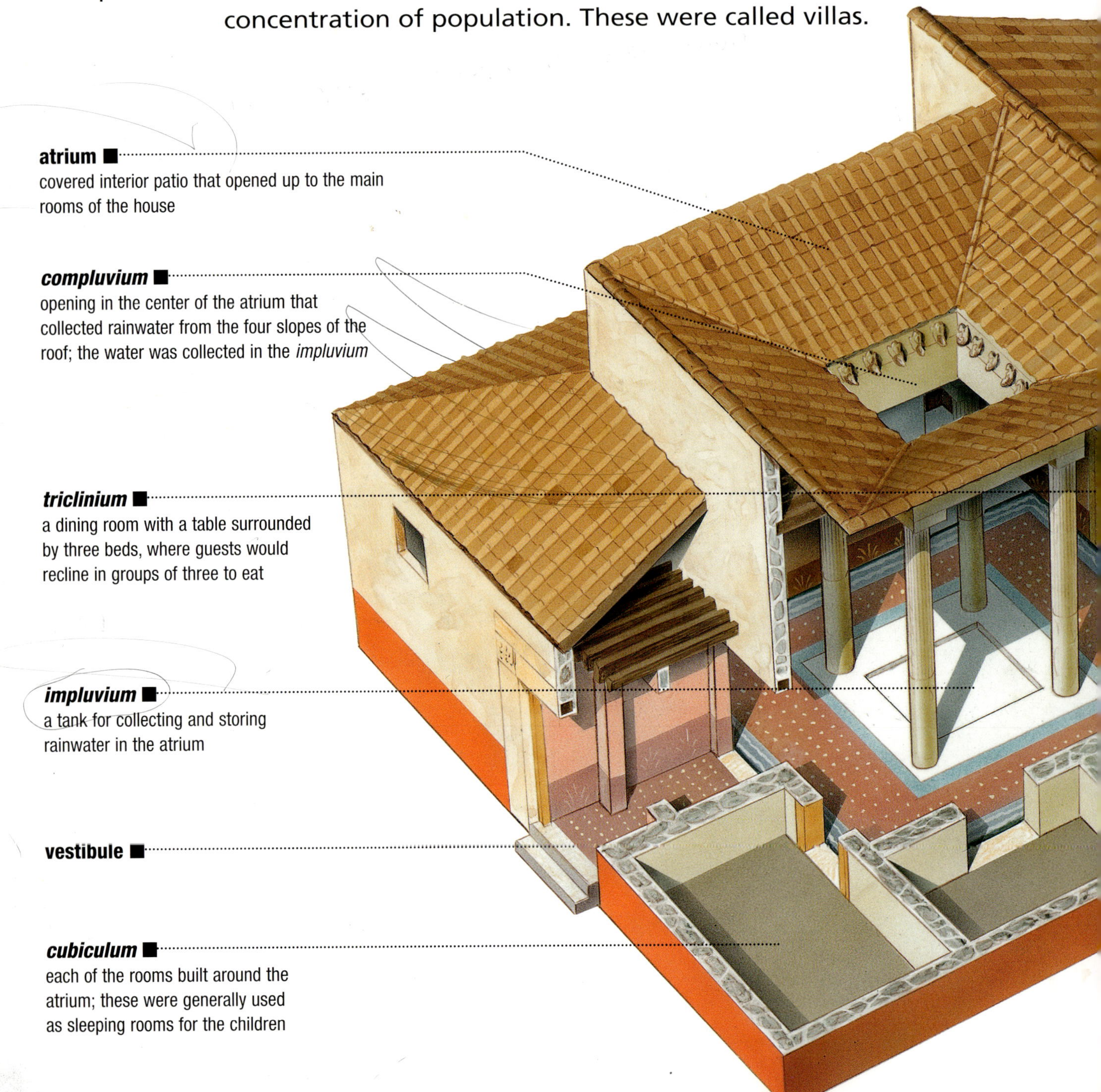

atrium
covered interior patio that opened up to the main rooms of the house

compluvium
opening in the center of the atrium that collected rainwater from the four slopes of the roof; the water was collected in the *impluvium*

triclinium
a dining room with a table surrounded by three beds, where guests would recline in groups of three to eat

impluvium
a tank for collecting and storing rainwater in the atrium

vestibule

cubiculum
each of the rooms built around the atrium; these were generally used as sleeping rooms for the children

INSULAS

In big cities such as Rome, *insulas* or housing blocks were constructed around a central patio with bricks and wooden beams: they could reach up to five floors in height. Taverns or different kinds of shops would be on the lower levels.

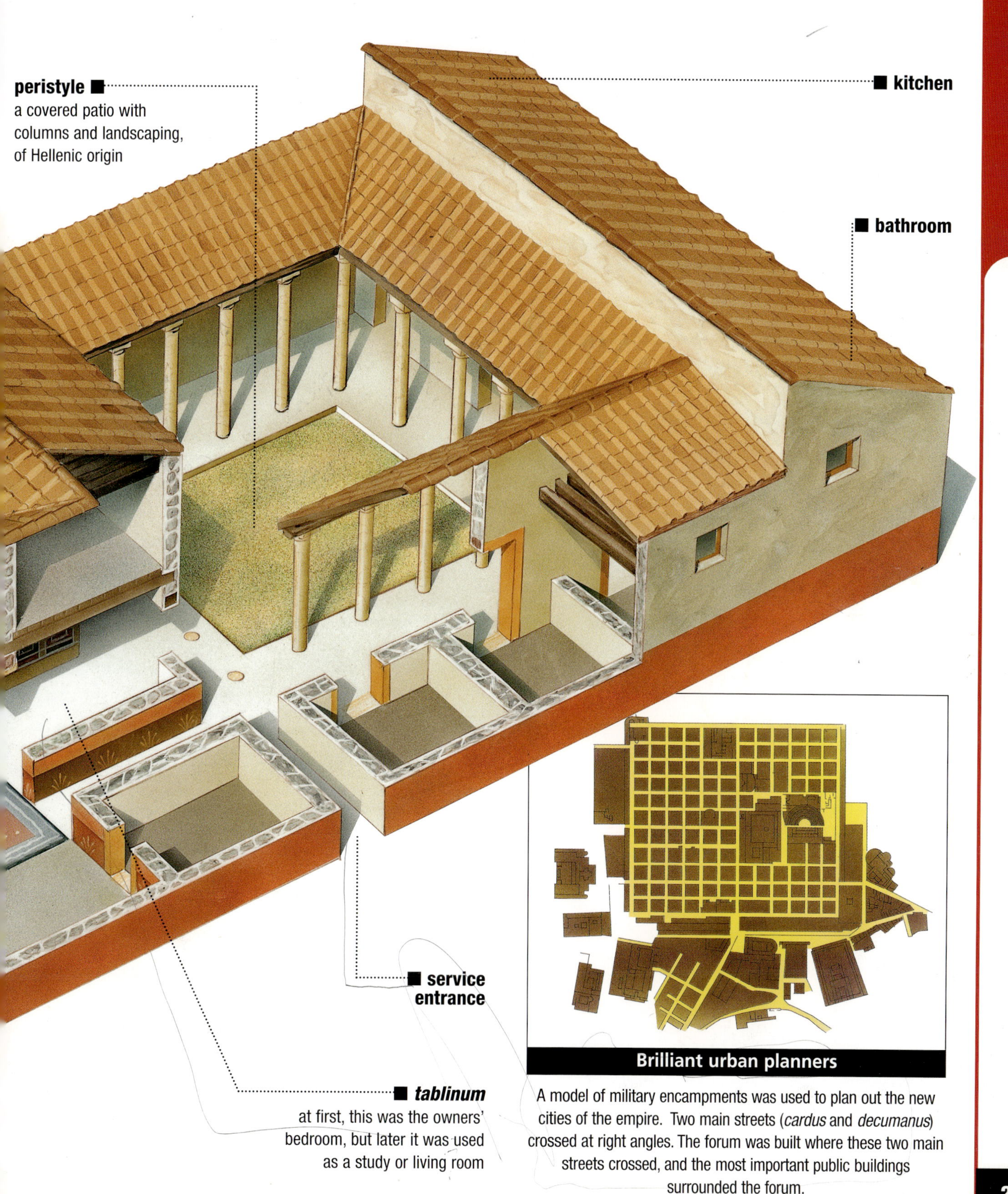

peristyle a covered patio with columns and landscaping, of Hellenic origin
kitchen
bathroom
service entrance
tablinum at first, this was the owners' bedroom, but later it was used as a study or living room

Brilliant urban planners

A model of military encampments was used to plan out the new cities of the empire. Two main streets (*cardus* and *decumanus*) crossed at right angles. The forum was built where these two main streets crossed, and the most important public buildings surrounded the forum.

BENEATH THE LAVA OF VESUVIUS

On August 29 in the year 79 A.D., a terrible catastrophe occurred: Mount Vesuvius suddenly erupted, and buried the city of Pompeii and its inhabitants, who had no time to escape, under a layer of ash and lava. Centuries later, archaeologists discovered beneath the lava a city that was nearly intact, with houses, taverns, a forum, several temples, an amphitheater, and the remains of a few villas. It was the decorations preserved in these residences that allowed art experts to study Roman painting, and to classify it into four styles or periods.

■ **Vesuvius**
an active volcano about 7.5 miles (12 kilometers) from Naples; the eruption of 79 A.D. buried the cities of Pompeii, Herculaneum, and Stabia; the last time Vesuvius erupted was in 1944

■ **Pliny the Elder**
Latin writer and scientist who died in Stabia, buried under the lava of Vesuvius, when he moved to the city to study the eruption up close

FROM RURAL FARMS TO SUMMER VILLAS

Originally, Roman villas, with structures similar to the *domus*, were centers of agricultural activity. However, with time, some of them became summer residences, and gradually genuine manors, surrounded by gardens and decorated with paintings and mosaics.

The mosaic

The decoration of floors and walls with mosaics was widely developed during Roman times. There were two basic techniques: the *opus tessellatum*, made of small tiles measuring less than half an inch on each side, and the *opus vermiculatum*, which used even smaller pieces.

■ **Herculaneum**
in this city, buried by the lava of Vesuvius, archaeologists discovered a library that contained more than eighteen hundred volumes

■ **Pompeii**
this ancient Roman city, which came to be home to more than twenty-five thousand people, served as a port for interior populations, and a place where well-to-do Romans had their second residences

■ **first pictorial style**
also called incrustation or structural because of its imitation of marble flagstones and columns

■ **second pictorial style**
called architectonic because it incorporated painted architectural elements that gave a certain perspective to the composition

■ **third pictorial style**
also known as the ornamental style because it recreates a fictitious architecture and false perspectives

■ **fourth pictoral style**
this last style was much more elaborate and recreated stage designs; it incorporated still lifes and marine landscapes in an architectural framework

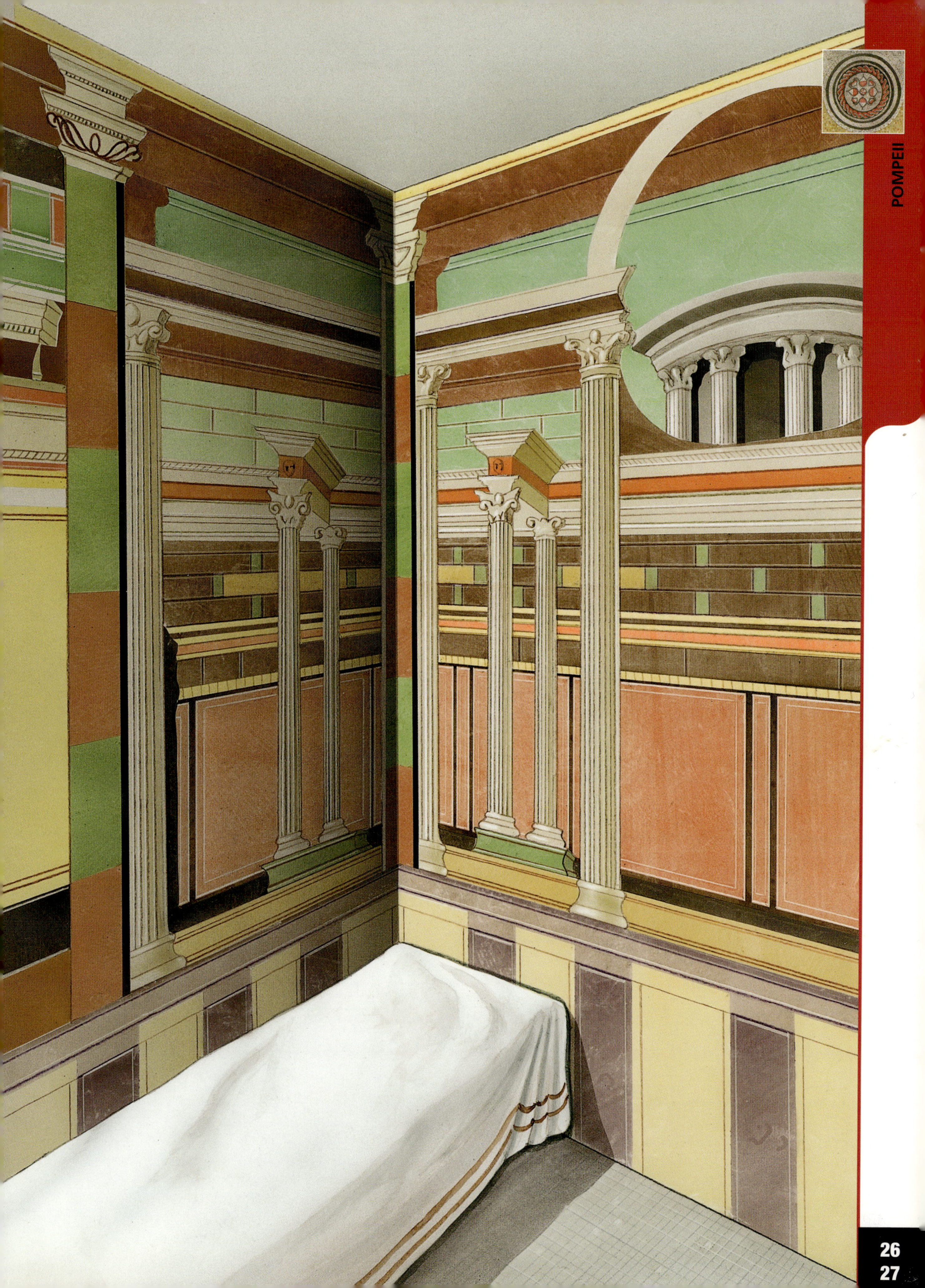

A GREAT EMPIRE, ONE LAW FOR ALL

Did you know that Roman law is still used as a point of reference for legal scholars and is still studied in law schools today? In the middle of the fifth century B.C., ten men were appointed to create a system of laws. Up until then laws had not been written down, but were transmitted orally. The laws were written on twelve tablets and displayed in the forum so that all citizens could see them. Basilicas were used as tribunals, places where citizens could present their legal claims.

Coins

The monetary system was as decisive an element as the law in the process of Romanization. Coins bearing an image of the emperor were minted. The most valuable coins were the *aureus*, a gold coin, and the *denarius*, made of silver.

■ ***decimvirs***
each one of the ten magistrates to whom the Romans entrusted the composition of the laws on twelve tablets

■ **common law**
laws that were not written down, but introduced by custom; they had been passed on by word of mouth from one generation to another

■ **invariable law**
written law, whose interpretation was the responsibility of magistrates acting as judges

■ **jurisprudence**
refers to interpretations that can be made of written laws

■ **jurists**
those charged with interpreting written laws; their decisions were later applied to similar cases that arose

THE ROMAN BASILICA

The first basilicas were large rectangular halls divided into naves by rows of columns, and sometimes crowned, on one or both ends, by apses. They were used as a tribunal, a marketplace, or a meeting center. With the advent of Christianity, they were adapted to celebrate religious ceremonies.

■ The Caracalla Reform
In the year 212 A.D., this emperor extended the right of citizenship to all the inhabitants of the empire; this way, the inhabitants of all the Roman provinces were judged by the same laws

■ public law
regulated the actions of citizens with respect to authority

■ private law
settled disputes and lawsuits between citizens

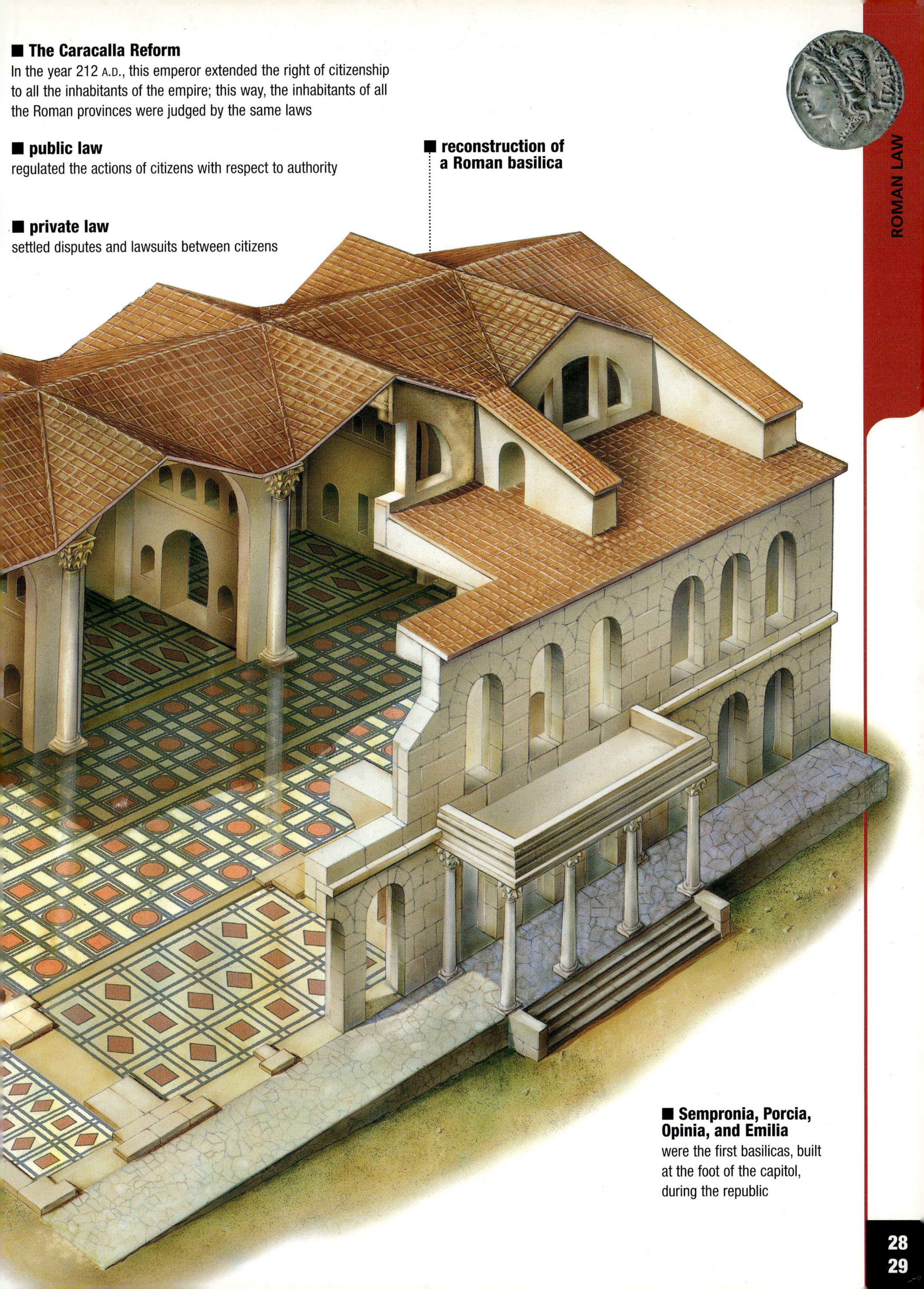
■ reconstruction of a Roman basilica

■ Sempronia, Porcia, Opinia, and Emilia
were the first basilicas, built at the foot of the capitol, during the republic

GLOSSARY

Baths Public areas used for bathing.

Cardus The main north-south artery in military camps and Roman cities.

Catacombs Underground galleries used by Jews and Christians in Rome for funerals.

Decumano Main east-west road in military encampments and Roman cities.

Forum The civic center of a city, generally located at the intersection of the two main streets, and around which are located the most representative buildings of the city government.

Incineration Cremation of a dead body.

Inhumation Burial of a dead body.

Insulas Housing blocks or groups of houses in the city.

Mortar Mixture of lime, sand, and water that is used in masonry.

Mint Place where coins are made.

Seating Total number of places or spectators in a theater or amphitheater.

CHRONOLOGY

753 B.C.	Beginning of the monarchy Founding of Rome
509 B.C.	Expulsion of the Etruscans from Rome Beginning of the Republic
264–241 B.C.	First Punic War
218–201 B.C.	Second Punic War
199 B.C.	Invasion of Macedonia
149–146 B.C.	Third Punic War
88 B.C.	Birth of the architect and treatise writer Vitruvius
59 B.C.	Julius Caesar is named consul
58–51 B.C.	Conquest of Gaul by Caesar
46–44 B.C.	Dictatorship of Caesar
30 B.C.	Death of Antony and Cleopatra
27 B.C.	Octavian is named Augustus
23 B.C.	Octavian Augustus is given imperial power
c. 15 B.C.	Foundation of Barcino (Barcelona)
12 B.C.	Augustus is named Pontifex Maximus (high priest)
14 A.D.	Tiberius, emperor
37	Caligula, emperor
41	Claudius, emperor
54	Nero, emperor
64	Fire of Rome
69	Vespasian, emperor Beginning of construction of the Roman Colosseum
79	Eruption of Vesuvius Destruction of Pompeii, Helculaneum, and Stabia Titus, emperor
81	Domitian, emperor
98	Trajan, emperor
117	Hadrian, emperor
118–125	Construction of the Roman Pantheon
161	Marcus Aurelius, emperor
193	Septimus Severus, emperor
212	Caracalla, emperor
284	Diocletian and Maximianus, emperors
307	Constantine and Maxentius, emperors
379	Theodosius, emperor
391	Christianity proclaimed official religion
410	Fall of Rome

FAMOUS PEOPLE

Julius Caesar	Great Roman statesman of the first century A.D. who instituted a triumvirate with Pompey and Crassus. Between 58 and 51 B.C., the conquest of the Gauls brought him great fame and glory. He crossed the Rubicon with his army and marched on Rome, unleashing a war against Pompey and the senate. In 44 B.C., he became consul and dictator of Rome for life. That same year, he was assassinated in the senate.
Octavian Augustus	Great-nephew of Caesar and emperor of Rome. With the name Augustus, came the powers that had been shared until then by different magistrates. He completed the conquest of Spain and brought the frontier of the empire up to the Danube River. After his death, he was named Pontifex Maximus, and was honored as a god.
Caligula	This Roman emperor, afflicted by mental disease, became a despot, and governed tyrannically until his death in the year 41.
Claudius	A cultured man, but weak in character, he was emperor from the year 41 until the year 54. His second wife, Agrippina, murdered him by giving him poison.
Nero	Adopted by the emperor Claudius, whom he succeeded, he carried out the first great persecution of the Christians, who were accused of the fire of Rome in the year 64. His suicide, four years later, put an end to a reign marked by terror and conspiracies.
Trajan	Born in Spain, he reigned between the years 98 and 117. During his rule, he fought against the Parthians and extended the borders of the Roman Empire to Arabia, Armenia, and Mesopotamia. He ordered the building of numerous monuments and buildings, including the forum that bears his name.
Hadrian	Successor of Trajan, he unified the legal system and defended the empire from the barbarians by ordering the construction of fortifications on the frontiers. Near Rome, he had a beautiful villa that bears his name. The building of a temple in Jerusalem dedicated to Jupiter provoked an uprising of the Jews in the year 134.
Caracalla	This Roman emperor is credited with promoting the edict that extended the right of Roman citizenship to the whole empire, and the construction in the City of Seven Hills of the baths that bear his name. He was assassinated near the Tigris River, on his way to fight the Parthians.
Diocletian	Proclaimed emperor in the year 284, nine years later he established the tetrarchy, in an effort to defend the empire better. He also carried out profound administrative, military, and judicial reforms. In the year 303, he ordered the persecution of Christians and other sects that did not accept the theocratic absolutism of the empire.
Constantine	This emperor, promoted an edict in 313 establishing freedom of religion, and also founded the city of Constantinople in ancient Byzantium.
Theodosius	Known as Theodosius the Great, he made Christianity the official religion of the empire and condemned paganism. When he died, the empire was divided between his two sons, Honorius and Arcadius.

INDEX